SCOTLAND IN COLOUR

SCOTLAND
in Colour

PHOTOGRAPHS BY KENNETH SCOWEN

INTRODUCTION BY FRED URQUHART

B. T. BATSFORD LTD. LONDON

First published, 1961

© Kenneth Scowen and Fred Urquhart, 1961

PRINTED AND BOUND IN DENMARK BY
F.E. BORDING LTD., COPENHAGEN AND LONDON
FOR THE PUBLISHERS
B.T. BATSFORD LTD.
4 FITZHARDINGE STREET, PORTMAN SQUARE, LONDON, W.I

CONTENTS

INTRODUCTION

'No country in Europe can offer so much variety as Scotland in so small a space.' Compton Mackenzie wrote that in 1932, and it still stands good. It should remain true as long as Scotland's natural beauties escape being covered by too many hideous pylons and rows of tasteless, coffin-shaped council houses – symbols of the twentieth century – and the individual traits of her people remain uncontaminated by the remorseless regimentation of the Welfare State. Not that either of these fates seems likely – for a long time, anyway. For, apart from the mining districts and the industrial belt of the Lowlands, Scotland is mainly an agricultural country; and the majority of Scots are too proud of their heritage to let themselves be dragooned into suburban robots. The Scottish emblem, the thistle, is prickly, and the old challenging roar of 'Whae daur meddle wi' me?' would probably still come from most Scottish throats at too much 'planned' interference in family or national life.

Scotland was an independent kingdom until 1603, when its king, James VI, also became James I of England and joined the two nations who had been at war with each other so often. This unification was only a theoretical one, however, and Scotland still retained her own laws until the Treaty of Union in 1707; a treaty that declared that the Scottish Cross of St. Andrew and the English Cross of St. George – the patron saints of the countries – were to be designed as one flag, and that there was to be one Parliament. The act of union more or less made Scotland the junior partner in this marriage of convenience, but actually she has retained much of her independence, and no doubt she will continue to assert this independence as long as Scots have breath left to cool their porridge. She still has certain laws that are different from English ones. In Scotland, for instance, you can attempt to commit suicide without any police prosecution following your lack of success. The verdicts in murder trials are not limited to Guilty and Not Guilty; there is a third verdict of Not Proven. And it is easier to get married quickly in Scotland than it is in England; hence the prevalence of runaway marriages to Gretna Green, safely on the Scottish side of the border.

Scotland is so indented by the sea that it covers an area of only 30,410 square miles. Its maximum length is 274 miles, and its maximum breadth 154 miles. Nearly 800 islands of the Inner and Outer Hebrides and the Orkneys and Shetlands surround the west and north coasts, and of these islands only 60 or so are more than 3 square miles in size. Many are uninhabited, for geographical or economic reasons. Large parts of the country are sparsely populated. Four-fifths of the entire population of not much more than 5,000,000 – the official figure at the 1951 census was 5,096,000 – are concentrated in the industrial belt of the Central Lowlands, one-fifth of them in Glasgow, the second city of what used to be the British Empire.

Besides the islands, Scotland is divided into two parts: the Highlands and the Lowlands. The Highlands are cut in halves by the Caledonian Canal, which stretches from the neighbourhood of Fort William in Argyllshire to Inverness, 60 miles away. Geographically, the Highlands also include the narrow strip of farming country between their foothills and the sea – a strip that starts from Sutherland in the north, circles the coast of the Moray Firth, and widens into the rich dairy and arable counties of Aberdeen and Kincardine in the northeast. The Lowlands are made up of the industrial belt between the Firths of Forth and Clyde; the dairy-farming counties of Dumfries, Galloway, and Ayrshire; the mining districts of Lanarkshire and Fifeshire; the agricultural area of the Lothians; and the sheep-rearing hills of the border counties, Roxburgh, Peebles, and Berwick.

8

This natural division of the country gives a great variety of scenery. The hills and rivers of the Lowlands are gentler and more pastoral than the turbulent rivers, rugged peaks, and grouse and deer moors of the Highlands. After travelling only a short distance, you might be in an entirely different country. A croft (small mountain farm) in Ross and Cromarty is quite unlike a farm in Perthshire. And although there may be surface resemblances between fishing villages on the northeast coast and those on the west coast, you will find them completely dissimilar if you stay long enough to study the fisherfolk and their habits.

Each of these districts has a tradition, dialect, characteristics, and outlook peculiarly its own. The dialects especially are varied. The visitor may think that everybody is speaking the same broad Scots, but he will find, if he listens carefully and compares the speech, that there are various inflections. Most Borderers speak with what is called a 'Berwickshire burr', a close cousin to the Northumberland burr across the Cheviot Hills. Although only 45 miles separate them, the Edinburgh tongue is totally unlike the Glasgow one, and even in these cities there are scales of intonation; in Glasgow you can always tell a native of the Gorbals from a native of the more 'refained' Kelvinside; and in Edinburgh there is a big difference between the accent of Leith and the High Street and that of Morningside, Kelvinside's twin sister of gentility in the capital. A soft-voiced farmer from Aberdeenshire or the Mearns calls a man 'a mannie' and a woman 'a wifie', and uses different words and phrases from those spoken by a farmer in the Rhinns of Galloway. The latter is likely to have an Irish tinge to his brogue, for this southeast part had close affinities with Ireland in the past. Apart from the speech of individual Scots who have been educated perhaps at English public schools, you will hear the purest English spoken in the Highlands, except that Highland voices have a lilt and are softer than most

English ones, and Highlanders have a propensity to pronounce 'b' as 'p' and 'j' as 'ch'.

There are still friendly rivalries among all these areas. Even if the days of the clan feuds and Highland cattle raiders are long distant and Highlanders are now welcomed in any Lowland village, the visitor must never make the mistake of assuming that a man from one district or town will be a blood-brother of, or have the same characteristics as, a man from a neighbouring one. You can offer no greater insult, for instance, than to ask an Edinburgh man if he belongs to Glasgow, or vice versa. I remember when I was a small boy hearing an old woman say with asperity to my grandfather, 'I may be a Highlander, Mr. Harrower, but I'm glad to say I'm not an Islander.' So be warned! It is better in all cases to let the Scot tell you first where he comes from and to discuss the question as little as possible, for fear of offending him.

The Scots are very touchy. Whatever you do, never try to imitate a Scotsman's accent. Some would-be comedians think it is very funny to greet all Scots with what is nothing more than a parody of the broadest Glasgow accent, an accomplishment they have learned from the least talented radio comedians. Let a Scot 'take a rise out of' his own accent and be 'a wee comic' as much as he likes. Some of us love to do it – especially for the benefit of strangers we want to impress – and we can put on wonderful performances. But never attempt to do it yourself.

Despite their reputation for dourness and rigid Calvinism, most Scots have a good sense of humour, and some are natural comedians. Considering this, it is strange that so few Scots music-hall comics achieved much success beyond the limits of their own country. Is this perhaps because they have overdone the pawkiness and used words that could be familiar only to native audiences? It is true that Harry Lauder and Will Fyffe entertained the world in their day, and most foreigners' conception of a Scot is based on Harry Lauder's wee bandy-legged man in a kilt. Two brilliant comediennes, Renée Houston and Molly Weir, have endeared themselves beyond the Border with their portraits of sharp-tongued Scottish wifies. But Harry Gordon, Dave Willis, and the late, great, and ever to be lamented Tommy Lorne (who had only to walk on a stage in Edinburgh or Glasgow, dressed as a pantomime dame, lift his hands helplessly, and say, 'In the name!' to make audiences howl with laughter) never captured non-Scottish audiences to any great extent.

You may have heard from some of these comedians that the Scots are pawky, thrifty, mean, and stiff-necked with pride. You may have heard also that they are inhospitable. But this, I can assure you, is not the case. Even T. W. H. Crosland could not accuse the Scots of inhospitality in *The Unspeakable Scot,* that diatribe in which he accused them of almost every vice under the sun. He particularly accused them of drunkenness, believing that the Scots drink whisky at every meal. And he told a story about spending one New Year's Eve with an Englishman married to a Scotswoman. 'At the sight of me', wrote Crosland, 'out of the bigness of her Scotch hospitality she proposed a "nip" and half filled three glasses. Then, with hand on hip, glass uplifted and a blaze on her face, she cried, "Here's tae us and – to hell with the English!"'

That happened over fifty years ago. No visitor from any land need worry that such a toast will be given today. A nip you will certainly get, if your host is lucky enough to have some of the hard stuff in the house, and probably you will get two or three. The Scots are almost effusive in their hospitality. They welcome visitors to their homes and never get tired of telling them about the beauty spots they must visit. They will go into such a wealth of detail that you may find yourself a bit confused by the spate of names, all apparently prefixed by 'Auch' or 'Glen'; but with the help of your proudly nationalist mentors you will be able to sort them out.

You may have heard that the Scots are so taciturn that they are mono-syllabic. Dinna believe it! You will realize how wrong this is after getting into conversation with one. In spite of all that has been said about their glum dourness, they are a gay, gregarious, and ebullient people, and most of them have long since discarded the pious mantles laid so heavily upon them by John Knox and his successors. Possibly you may come across a couple of old men or women having a conversation that seems to consist mainly of nods, punctuated by 'Ays' and 'Imphms'. But mostly you will find that even if you just ask the way of the dourest-looking Scot, he will be only too delighted to give you helpful advice (because it is cheap!), and you will be lucky if he doesn't describe half a dozen alternate routes and insist on coming part of the way with you.

In fact, if you ask the way of anybody in Glasgow he will convoy you right to your destination. The Glaswegians are famed for their gregarious-ness. A story is told about this in Janet Dunbar's biography of Dame Flora Robson, the celebrated actress, who, although born in England, is of Scot-tish parentage. On one of her first visits to the land of her fathers, the actress needed a pair of shoes to match the dress she wore in the play *Dangerous Corner* by J. B. Priestley, and she and Lady Sibyl Colefax, the artistic director of the company, boarded a street-car in Glasgow to go to buy them. The tram was crowded, and Dame Flora and her companion had to strap-hang. The other passengers stared at them and asked questions with inquisitive frankness, and soon everybody knew who they were and where they were going. So that when they arrived at their stop the entire tramload shouted, 'Here ye are! He–rre ye are!'

Before going to Scotland you may have some preconceived notions about its scenery and people. It is better to drop these at the start. You may, for instance, have seen films with Scottish stories and backgrounds. You will probably find that the scenery is grander than any you have seen on the screen, and you will certainly meet nobody who either behaves or speaks like most of the actors in the 'Scots' parts. I have scarcely ever seen a film in which the Scots were not caricatured. A friend in the film industry affirms that Scotland is the kiss of death as far as films are concerned. It would be more correct to say that films have put the kiss of death on Scotland! Some documentaries, such as John Grierson's *Night Mail* and *Drifters,* and an occasional comedy like *Whisky Galore* have shown interesting sides of the country and its people, but some of Hollywood's 'historical' epics are such travesties that they are best forgotten. No Scot will ever forgive them – especially a version of the life of Mary, Queen of Scots, in which the handsome actor playing the Earl of Bothwell stood in one scene in front of a fire, lifting his kilt to warm himself, and said in a strong American accent to one of the Queen's four Maries that he'd give her a spank where it belonged!

If you want to get some idea of the tragic life of Mary Stuart, it is better to visit the places where she lived and loved. And nowhere could be a better starting point than the Palace of Holyroodhouse in Edinburgh.

Edinburgh is large enough to maintain its prestige as a capital city, yet it is small enough, compact enough, to let you view all its historical buildings and monuments in a fairly short time. You can, if you are rushed, do it in a day, though I don't advise this. In the morning you can visit the Castle, with its dungeons, Queen Margaret's Chapel, the Crown Room, the Banqueting Hall, and the scene of many dark, bloody, and noble deeds. The Scottish National War Shrine, evoking memories of more recent and bloodier wars, is set in its heart. From the battlements on its rock you can see the panoramic sweep of the city and the Firth of Forth, the Fifeshire coast and the Pentland Hills, and the sedate crawl of traffic along Princes Street. And perhaps on the wide esplanade you may be lucky enough to see a military ceremony, with all the pomp of swirling kilts and martial bagpipes, performed by whichever Scottish regiment is stationed at the Castle at the time. A leisurely walk from the Castle, down the 'Royal Mile' of the High Street with its closes and vennels and old houses, where the Scots aristocracy used to live, will lead you past the Heart of Midlothian, set in cobbles beside St. Giles' Cathedral, and John Knox's house, until you come to Holyrood Palace, with the hill of Arthur's Seat towering above it. The room where Mary's Italian secretary, Rizzio, was murdered; the Queen's bedroom; Darnley's apartments; the vast picture gallery; and the ruins of Holyrood Abbey – all these can be seen in an hour or two, although their romantic atmosphere should lead you to imaginative reconstructions of the past that will linger in your mind for a long time.

An afternoon can be spent in visiting the University, founded in 1582, and the Scottish National Gallery, but it leaves little time to see any of the historical buildings of the New Town, particularly the museum in Queen Street and the old gaol on the Calton Hill. Edinburgh is rich in literary associations, and Scott, Burns, Stevenson, Thomas Carlyle, and countless others have left their mark on the old grey stones. If you visit the city at the time of the annual Festival of Music and Dramatic Art – now a highlight of Edinburgh's year – you can blend the old culture and the new. If you do, perhaps you could look in at the Abbotsford, a pub or 'howff' in Rose Street, where many of the modern Scottish writers gather. On any evening there you might see the poets Hugh MacDiarmid, Norman MacCaig, Sydney Goodsir Smith (whose play in verse, *The Wallace,* was a feature of the 1960 Festival) and the playwrights Alexander Reid and Robert Kemp.

Edinburgh is an excellent centre for planning your itinerary of Scotland.

It is within easy reach of the Walter Scott country of the Borders. Day trips can be made to the Trossachs, as well as to Perthshire and Fifeshire, though of course neither of these counties can be seen or appreciated in a short time. Besides the gorgeous scenery of Perthshire, you must not miss the town of Perth itself, or Scone, the ancient coronation place of Scottish kings, from which Edward I removed the Stone of Destiny to Westminster Abbey in 1297. And in Fifeshire do not forget Dunfermline, the old capital, or St. Andrews with its ruined cathedral, a lasting reminder of its associations with the Reformation, and the oldest Scottish university, founded in 1411. It was in St. Andrews that John Knox preached his first sermon, and it was on the surrender of the castle, after a siege of a year, that he was sent to France to endure nineteen months as a galley-slave. If your inclinations are neither academic nor historical, St. Andrews offers you golf on its 'Royal and Ancient' course, one of the finest and best-known courses in the world.

But perhaps you would prefer to make Glasgow your headquarters for your Scottish trip. It is a handy jumping-off place for the West Highlands, within easy reach of Oban, Fort William, and other centres; and from it you can make steamer trips to the island of Arran and the Kyles of Bute. The Firth of Clyde is not only famous for its shipbuilding; it is a yachts-man's paradise. Like Edinburgh, Glasgow is handy for the Trossachs – Loch Lomond is a favourite day-trip for holiday-bent Glaswegians anxious to rid themselves of the smoke and grime of factories and shipyards – as well as for Stirling, where the castle, standing on an impregnable rock, rivals that of Edinburgh for beauty and romance. Glasgow is also well situated for jaunts to Burns'-haunted Ayrshire, particularly places like Maybole and Mauchline, which will always be identified with the youth of 'rantin', roarin' Rab,' and the cottage at Alloway where he was born, which lures thousands of Burns' admirers every year.

15

Glasgow was founded by St. Mungo when he went there about A.D. 543 to preach Christianity to the natives of Strathclyde. Little is known of its history until 1136, when Bishop John Achaius consecrated a church on the site of the present cathedral, and apparently it remained not much more than an obscure village until its university was founded in 1450. Since then, however, Glasgow has 'flourished', as its natives say, growing with the help of its shipbuilding and other industries to its present size. As a city, it has not as many romantic traditions and historic associations as Edinburgh, but it is a friendly place, reminding one of an exuberant overgrown youth unaware of his own strength, and it welcomes visitors to its vast, whisky-soaked bosom. Its long streets sprawl over a tremendous area, and even if most of them are architecturally ugly and uninteresting, you won't really notice their aesthetic lack because of the gay charm of their inhabitants. Many of Glasgow's finest and oldest buildings were destroyed or otherwise mutilated by the city's expansion after the Industrial Revolution, among them the Old College in High Street; the university moved to larger premises on Gilmore-hill. The cathedral, too, was denuded of its western tower and fifteenth-century consistory house by Council and Church 'planners' a century ago. However, Glasgow still retains a number of fine buildings, including the School of Art, designed by Charles Rennie Mackintosh.

Artistically, Glasgow has not fallen far behind Edinburgh. The Glasgow School of Painters flourished in the late nineteenth century, paving the way for its artists of today. And John Galt's and Walter Scott's portrayals of old Glasgow worthies have been rivalled in the present century in the novels and stories of George Blake, James Barke, Edward Gaitens, and Robin Jenkins. Glasgow has also produced one playwright of international reputation in James Bridie.

The city's Hampden Park, the largest football arena in Britain and one of the largest in the world, will remind you that traditionally Scotland is the birthplace of football. In ancient days it vied with golf as the national game, and it is said that some of the retainers of Mary, Queen of Scots, played a game to keep her mind off the outcome of the Battle of Langside. Football is what George Blake has called 'the national obsession,' and if you are in Glasgow on a Saturday, when there is a match between the Celtic and the Rangers, you will find the whole of the masculine population in such a ferment that you could be forgiven for thinking that a war had started.

After Edinburgh and Glasgow, Scotland's two largest cities are Aberdeen and Dundee.

If you go from Edinburgh to Aberdeen by car you can take in Dundee on the way. Or you can go by train along the east coast and enter the city over the Tay Bridge. Whichever way you go, Dundee is certainly worth a visit. Today it is mainly a manufacturing town, being the centre of the linen and jute industry, as well as making marmalade and confectionery, but, like most Scots towns of its strategic importance, it has a historic past. Dundee was held by the English during the time of Edward I, and besieged by Sir William Wallace, who called off the siege, however, to march to meet the relieving English army at the Battle of Stirling Bridge, a battle which he won and which freed Scotland from the English yoke for a brief period. It was again besieged in 1651 by one of Cromwell's generals, Monck, and there was such a massacre of the inhabitants afterwards that no other Scots town dared to oppose the Roundhead victor. In 1543, George Wishart returned to Scotland from exile and started to preach the doctrine of the Reformation in Dundee – an act which led eventually to his being burned at the stake in St. Andrews, in front of the palace of Cardinal Beaton, who lay on velvet cushions while watching Wishart's martyrdom.

The road from Dundee to Aberdeen passes along the coast of the North Sea, through the towns of Arbroath, Montrose, Bervie, and Stonehaven. This cold, bleak landscape is called the Mearns, and its red soil is excellent for farming. Near Bervie is the village of Drumlithie, and on a farm in that neighbourhood in the early years of this century lived a boy named James Leslie Mitchell. He was educated at the Mackie Academy in Stonehaven, and when he grew up he published three novels about that district under the pen-name of Lewis Grassic Gibbon. If you would understand the minds and characters of the people of the Mearns, you must read *Sunset Song, Cloud Howe,* and *Grey Granite,* which have been published collectively as *A Scots Quair.* Grassic Gibbon died in 1935, at the age of thirty-four, but his lively, inquiring mind and great knowledge of and sympathy with the earthy farming folk of the northeast still live in the racy pages of his trilogy. It is one of the greatest Scottish books of the twentieth century.

And so we come to Aberdeen, the third city of Scotland, a place of great antiquity lying between the mouths of the rivers Dee and Don. It has a population of nearly 200,000, many of them fishing people. It is the chief Scottish centre of the white-fishing industry, and although this means an early morning rise, you must visit the great fishmarket. It is a sight not to be missed. Here through the night the trawlers unload their catch, and frequently miles of haddock, cod, halibut, turbot, and other varieties of fish lie waiting at dawn for the auctioneers. After the bustle of the fishmarket, you will probably be glad to relax and walk slowly through the wide streets of the city and admire its glistening white granite buildings. Aberdeen is sometimes called 'the Silver City by the Sea', sometimes 'the Granite City', and much of its wealth has come from this stone. About 1764 granite was found to be ideal for paving the streets of London, and that was the beginning of the Aberdeen granite trade, making the local stonemason unequalled. In his fascinating book *North-East Lowlands of Scotland,* John R. Allan, a native of Aberdeenshire, records that nearly sixty years ago 'it was quite common for Aberdeen masons to go to the United States in the spring, work there till the fall and then return to their families in the winter.'

Besides being a clean, pleasant, and prosperous place, Aberdeen is one of the most cultured in Great Britain. The Cathedral of St. Machar was erected in the fourteenth century. King's College or University of Old Aberdeen was founded by Bishop William Elphinstone in 1495; later it was expanded by the building of Marischal College, which proud Aberdonians claim as the finest granite building in the world. Graduates of Aberdeen University are to be found in most of the professions, and among those who have enriched Scottish literature in this century are Rachel Annand Taylor, Agnes Muir Mackenzie, Gordon Daviot, Neil M. Gunn, Eric Linklater, G. S. Fraser, and Neil Paterson. Lord Byron was educated at the Grammar School, and many other famous Scots had affiliations with the city.

No visit to Aberdeen is complete without a trip along Deeside, that lovely stretch of country which has become so popular with tourists since the Prince Consort rebuilt Balmoral Castle for Queen Victoria in 1854. Now the favourite summer residence of the British Royal family, the Castle is near the village of Braemar, where the Highland Gathering or Games is an annual and most colourful attraction. In recent years the Gathering has developed into a commercialized picture-postcard scene. Many of the tartans are not authentic, the Scots antecedents of their wearers are dubious, and there are too many professional he-men tossing the caber and simpering lovelies doing Highland Flings that are more like can-cans. In fact, it is more like a Hollywood conception of Highland Games than a Scottish one. Nevertheless, if you are in the neighbourhood at the time, you should see it.

North of Aberdeen are the fishing ports of Peterhead (which enjoys doubtful celebrity because of its huge prison), Fraserburgh, Macduff, Buckie, and Lossiemouth, birthplace of James Ramsay MacDonald, first Socialist Prime Minister of Britain. You go through them and many smaller fishing villages if you want to drive along the coast from Aberdeen to Inverness. If you want to see the Cairngorm Mountains, however, another road to Inverness goes through Tomintoul, the highest village in Scotland, Bridge of Brown, and Grantown-on-Spey. Near Grantown, if you cut away from the main road, a few miles will take you to Culloden Moor, the scene of the defeat in 1745 of Prince Charles Edward Stuart, the Young Pretender, by Hanoverian forces commanded by the Duke of Cumberland. A large stone cairn commemorates this collapse of the Stuart cause, and there are huge mounds where Charles's faithful Highlanders are buried, with stones to mark their clans. It is a desolate, eerie spot, evocative of bloodshed and betrayal, and if you are very sensitive and imaginative, it might perhaps be better to give it a miss.

No matter from which way you approach the Highlands, you are bound to touch Inverness. It is sometimes called the capital of the Highlands, and in olden days its castle was a residence of Scottish kings. It is situated at the head of the River Ness, at the north end of the Great Glen (a natural part of the Caledonian Canal), and its surroundings are beautiful beyond description. At one time, when Highland lairds lived on their estates, Inverness was a social meeting-place for them and their families. But, since most of the lairds have moved to London, it is only at the height of the shooting season now that Inverness regains some of its former aristocratic glories.

What can I say about the magnificence of the Highlands that you cannot see for yourself from the photographs that follow? It would be useless to attempt to describe the individual glens, moors, and mountains, for I would run out of superlatives and you would get tired of the repetition of the ad-

20

jectives 'superb', 'grand', 'spectacular', and 'awe-inspiring'. The Highlands have been praised so often by great poets that who am I to try to rival them? All I can say is: Come to the Highlands and see them for yourself. You will not go away unrewarded, and the likelihood is that you will return to see them again and again; and each time you will take away some new and fascinating memory of their grandeur.

In 1763 the great Dr. Samuel Johnson, around whom the literary life of London revolved, met a young Scotsman named James Boswell. At this period Scotsmen were hated in England because the Prime Minister, John Stuart, Earl of Bute, was always appointing fellow Scots to important positions in political and public life; and in his *London Journal* Boswell relates that, when two Highland officers entered the stalls in Covent Garden Opera House one evening, the mob in the uppper gallery pelted them with apples and shouted: 'No Scots! No Scots! Out with them!' Boswell knew that Dr. Johnson also had what he called 'a mortal antipathy' to Scotsmen (though the hated Bute was responsible later for giving him a pension), so when he was introduced to him by Mr. Davies in Russell Street, he cried: 'Don't tell him where I come from'. 'However, he said, "From Scotland". "Mr. Johnson", said I, "indeed I come from Scotland, but I cannot help it". "Sir", replied he, "that I find, is what a very great many of your countrymen cannot help".' Nevertheless, Dr. Johnson appears to have got over this prejudice, and ten years later he and Boswell set off on a trip to the West Highlands and Islands. The result was the publication of Johnson's own *Journey to the Western Isles of Scotland* in 1775, and Boswell's *Journal of a Tour to the Hebrides* in 1785, a book that is now more widely read than the Doctor's. Their friendship also led to the writing of Boswell's classic *Life of Dr. Johnson.*

It is hardly likely that, if you come to Scotland, you will come with any of Dr. Johnson's prejudices. If you had them, probably you would not trouble to come at all. The very fact that you are considering a visit to the country means that half the battle is won. So I will end this short, and unfortunately inadequate, introduction to the beautiful scenery and romantic traditions of wild Caledonia by trying to give a few more generalizations about the people you are going to meet.

The Scots are a heterogeneous people. The Highlanders are Celts, but the Lowlanders are of mixed Anglo-Saxon, Irish, and Scandinavian ancestry. The Norse invasions left their mark on the country, and despite the old feuds, Highlanders and Lowlanders have often intermarried. So don't be surprised to find some small, dark Celtic-looking Lowlanders as well as tall red-haired ones, and tall blond Vikings of Highlanders as well as dour dark ones. The Auld Alliance gave the Scots tongue many a French cast (for instance, a large meat plate in Scotland is called an ashet, presumably from *l'assiette*), and two Polish invasions have added more foreign blood to both language and physiognomy. The first Polish invasion was that of Polish miners who came to work in the Scottish coal-pits in the nineteenth century; the second was the stationing of Polish troops in the country during the 1939-45 war. Many Polish soldiers married Scots girls and remained in their adopted country after the war, so that in time, no doubt, you will meet Scots with names even more difficult to pronounce than their present ones.

The Scots are shipbuilders, farmers, fishermen, coalminers, scholars, lawyers, and engineers. They are golfers and footballers. Some Scots are thrifty, some are so extravagant that they gaily throw their bonnets over the windmill. They are proud, ambitious, passionate, and parsimonious. They are cautious, reckless, solemn, and gregarious. They have been Reformers and Covenanters. They have been – and still are – bonny fighters. And, although most of them love their native land this side of idolatry, they have been great emigrants. The High Road to England has always been waiting for the hobnailed boots of every village 'lad o' pairts', with London as his Mecca. The adventurous spirit of the Scots has led them in thousands upon thousands to Canada, New Zealand, Australia, and many other distant lands, to set up new homes.

Perhaps you are descended from one of them? Perhaps you have already heard the glories of Scotland sung and spun into endless yarns on farms in Manitoba or Kansas or New South Wales; or in homes in Ottawa, New York, Brisbane, and Dunedin? If you have, what can I say that will be new to you?

If you have not heard all this before, you will discover it for yourself when you come to the country. And you will find much more besides. As well as enchanting scenery you will find a highly individual and warm-hearted people, eager to welcome you, not for the money you bring but for yourself.

But now it is time for the pictures to lure you away. I hope they will persuade you to come to Scotland. I hope, too, that you will enjoy your visit, and that you will come again and come often.

Fred Urquhart

Edinburgh: Scott Monument in East Princes Street Gardens

Visitors to Edinburgh have their own favourite memories or pictures. Some are enchanted by the Palace of Holyrood, haunted by Mary, Queen of Scots; the Castle on its rock above the city; and the 'Royal Mile' of history that separates them. Others prefer the Georgian style of the New Town and its associations with Scott and Robert Louis Stevenson. But all are impressed by Princes Street, one of the most beautiful thoroughfares in Europe, which effectively divides the Old Town from the New.

The Castle, dominating Princes Street, recalls that Edinburgh's early name was Dunedin–'The Fort on the Hill Slope'–and that, according to tradition, it was founded a thousand years before the Christian era by King Edbranke, who also founded the city of York. But the eye can't avoid the Scott Monument, evidence of man's desire to emulate nature. This conical edifice, rising to over 200 feet in a series of diminishing arches, was built over a hundred years ago. Its architect, George Kemp, a Peeblesshire man, saw Sir Walter twice but never met him. In the foreground the statue of David Livingstone is a reminder that the Scots are also missionaries and explorers.

24

Culross

      Culross, a picturesque old town on the estuary of the Forth several miles west of the Forth Bridge, was made a Royal Burgh by James VI in 1588. From the water, its crooked narrow streets and wynds, with cottages set at curious angles to them, rise steeply to the ruins of its ancient grey Abbey and its red-tiled 'palace' or 'place', now in the keeping of the Scottish National Trust.

St. Serf, who converted Fife to Christianity in the sixth century, founded a church here, and it was the birthplace of St. Mungo, the patron saint of Glasgow. In olden days it was a favourite resort of Scottish kings. Later it was a busy port, trading in salt and coal, and was famous for the making of 'girdles' for baking scones. But its great days of profit-making have gone with its courtiers and burgesses, and now its old-world charm is untainted by modern industrialisation.

Callander and the River Teith

Callander, a pretty little town, lies at the entrance to the Highlands through the Pass of Leny. Above it rises Ben Ledi, 'The Hill of God', on the summit of which the Druids used to light their Beltane altar. Good salmon and trout fishing can be had in the Teith, a clear, fast-running river, one branch of which comes from Rob Roy's country, the Braes of Balquhidder, and the other which rises in Glengyle and goes through Lochs Katrine and Achray.

Near Callander are Dunblane Cathedral, praised by Ruskin and probably one of the finest in the world; the field of the Battle of Sheriffmuir (1715); and the magnificent ruin of Doune Castle, a stronghold erected in the fourteenth century by the Duke of Albany, regent of Scotland, and the residence later of the 'Bonnie Earl of Moray' of ballad fame.

West of Callander the road leads to the Trossachs.

Loch Katrine in the Trossachs

The Trossachs, immortalised in Scott's *Rob Roy* and *The Lady of the Lake,* are a 'Highlands in miniature'. All those who come to see Ellen's Isle, the hiding place of bygone *caterans,* or Highland robbers, and the refuge of the banished Douglas, will remember Fitz James's first impressions:

> *One burnish'd sheet of living gold,*
> *Loch Katrine lay beneath him roll'd.*

In 1803, seven years before the publication of Scott's poem, the district was visited by Wordsworth and his sister, accompanied by Samuel Taylor Coleridge. Dorothy, describing a sail on the loch, wrote: 'I can impart but little of what we felt . . . It was an entire solitude; and all that we beheld was the perfection of loveliness and beauty.'

This loveliness and beauty still remain, but the solitude has gone with the commercialisation of the region since it was 'discovered' by Scott and the Wordsworths.

30

Falls of Dochart, Killin, Perthshire

The village of Killin is at the western end of Loch Tay. Before the River Dochart tumbles into the waters of the loch, it flows round a dark, rocky islet, the ancient burial ground of the chiefs of the Clan Macnab. It is a sombre spot even on a sunny day. Near at hand are Kinnell House, the one-time home of the chiefs, and the ruins of Finlarig Castle, built in 1523 by Black Duncan of the Cowl, an ancestor of the Breadalbane family whose estates used to stretch for miles–at one time a hundred in one direction–over this area. The castle is mentioned in *The Fair Maid of Perth*. Fingal, the Celtic hero of Ossian's poems, is buried outside the village.

From the bridge there is a view of the wide valley of the Dochart, and Ben More (3,843 ft.) can be seen on a fine day.

Loch Faskally, near Pitlochry, Perthshire

Faskally is a man-made 'loch', constructed in recent years by the North of Scotland Hydro-Electric Board at the junction of the rivers Garry and Tummel, two miles north west of Pitlochry. It takes its name from the estate and mansion of Faskally.

Although Pitlochry has little history of its own, it is set in the midst of historic scenes. It has grown from a tiny clachan or hamlet into one of Scotland's most fashionable resorts and now runs a Festival Theatre each summer. Within easy reach is the village of Kinnaird, where Robert Louis Stevenson wrote *Thrawn Janet* and *The Merry Men*.

Beyond Pitlochry is the narrow Pass of Killiecrankie, where a fierce battle took place in 1689 between the troops of William of Orange and the Highlanders under the command of 'Bonnie Dundee' (Graham of Claverhouse), who had raised the standard of the exiled King James VII and II.

Glen Moriston looking towards Kintail

From Invermoriston on the shores of Loch Ness, this wide and gracious glen stretches westward to the Clunie Hills. Glen Moriston's historical past is as spectacular as its scenery. St. Columba visited it about A.D. 565 and probably founded the old church at Invermoriston. Columba's Well in its vicinity was noted for many centuries for its curative properties. In 1384, King Robert II granted the lands of this glen and neighbouring Glen Urquhart to his son, Alexander, Earl of Buchan, a wild lawless character known as 'The Wolf of Badenoch'. During the imprisonment of Mary, Queen of Scots in Lochleven Castle, the sum of £172 was assigned from the feu-duties of these glens to meet her expenses. After Culloden, Bonnie Prince Charlie was sheltered for three weeks in a cave by the Seven Men of Glen Moriston while Cumberland's men ravaged the district, searching for him. Although there was a reward of £30,000 for the Young Pretender, nobody betrayed him.

Glen Affric

A road runs up from Invercannich in Glen Urquhart to Glen Affric, a glen considered by many to be the most beautiful in the Highlands. Overlooking its pine and birch forests and its lochs are the mountains, Mam Sodhail (3,862 ft.) and–beyond the upper tributaries of the River Affric–Sgurr nan Ceathreahmnan, from the summit of which can be seen one of the most wonderful panoramas in the country. Horatio McCulloch (1805–1867), in his time a popular landscape painter, was probably the first artist to be attracted by this part of the Highlands. Besides his 'Glen Affric', his paintings of Glencoe, Loch Lomond and Loch Maree can still be admired.

Loch A' Chroisg and Scuir Vuillin, Ross and Cromarty

Not far from Dingwall, an ancient Royal Burgh on the Cromarty Firth, is the spa of Strathpeffer, famous for its medicinal springs and known as 'the Harrogate of the North'. The road from Strathpeffer leads westward, past the Falls of Rogie, to the village of Achnasheen, with its forked roads leading to Strome Ferry and Skye in one direction and Loch Maree in the other.

On the road to Kinlochewe, at the head of Loch Maree, you pass the clear waters of Loch A' Chroisg, in which are reflected the dark slopes of Scuir Vuillin (2,778 ft.).

Loch Maree and Ben Slioch, Ross and Cromarty

Legend-haunted Maree is eighteen miles long and at one time was joined to Loch Ewe, the sea loch. Its surface is dotted by over twenty small wooded islands. On one of these, Eilean Maree, are the ruins of a monastery and a Culdee cell, said to have been founded by St. Maree from Iona, and the graves of a Norse prince and princess whose lives ended in tragedy. It also contains a sacred well, described by Whittier in his poem on the loch: a well to which the insane were brought in olden times to lave their brows and be cured.

The loch is renowned for its salmon and sea-trout fishing. The rocky slopes of Ben Slioch (over 3,000 ft.) sometimes give its waters a gloomy, mysterious air in keeping with its legends.

River Inver and Quinag, Sutherland

The River Inver issues from the west end of Loch Assynt and flows south-west through splendid mountain scenery to Loch Inver, a sea loch. At its estuary lies the little town of Lochinver.

During the English Civil War, the great Marquis of Montrose, still fighting desperately for the Stuart cause against Cromwell's troops, spent his last weeks in this neighbourhood. He was eventually captured by Macleod of Assynt in 1650 and taken, starving, to Ardvreck Castle, the ruins of which now stand on a peninsula in Loch Assynt.

Montrose's journey to his execution in Edinburgh is movingly told in Neil M. Gunn's fine short story *Montrose Rides By*.

Loch Cairnbawn with Quinag, Sutherland

Quinag, the highest mountain in this area (2,653 ft.), is a desolate massed hump with no sign of life or vegetation, although the golden eagle of the Highlands probably still finds a home in its craggy fastness. It lies between Loch Assynt and Loch Cairnbawn, a sea loch to its north. Near the junction of Cairnbawn and two other sea lochs, Glendhu and Glencoul, there is a village called Unapool, which should not be confused with Ullapool, an attractive little town with a fairly busy harbour on Loch Broom, about twenty-five miles south as the golden eagle flies.

Eilean Donan Castle, Rossshire

      Eilean Donan Castle, an ancient fortress on a rocky islet at the meeting place of three sea-inlets, Loch Duich, Loch Long and Loch Alsh – 'the Gateway to the Hebrides' – lies beneath the shadows of the mountains called the Five Sisters of Kintail. It is 'one of the wildest and loveliest scenes in the west', wrote J. J. Bell, author of *Wee Macgregor* and other books that were popular in their time. In 1539 the castle was held by two men and a youth against a fleet of galleys. From nearby Dornie the road goes to the Kyle of Lochalsh, where there is a ferry across the mile of water to Kyleakin on the Island of Skye.

Skye, looking south across Portree Harbour

Skye, the second largest of Scotland's islands, was called 'Isle of Mist' by Ossian, and it could have no better name, for a fine drizzle or 'Scotch mist' often obscures its beauties. Its association with Prince Charles and Flora Macdonald have been celebrated in story and song ever since she brought him there in the summer of 1746, disguised as her maid 'Betty Burke'.

In 1773, Dr. Johnson and James Boswell visited Skye on their tour of the Hebrides, slept at Kingsburgh House in the room once occupied by the Prince, and met Flora Macdonald, 'a little woman, of a genteel appearance, and uncommonly mild and well-bred'. She died in 1790, aged 68, and was buried in Kilmuir kirkyard, her coffin being followed by over 3,000 mourners.

Portree, the chief town, is a suitable base for visits to all parts, but some people may prefer to make their headquarters at Broadford, several miles farther south and nearer to Kyleakin.

Dunvegan Castle, Skye

Dunvegan, the ancient castle of the Macleods, is still lived in by the chief of the clan, whose ancestry goes back to the Norse kings of the Isle of Man. It is twenty-three miles from Portree, and is washed on three sides by the sea.

Among its treasures is the Fairy Flag, a piece of faded yellow silk embroidered by red spots. One tradition holds that this was taken from a Saracen chief during the Crusades; another maintains that it belonged to a fairy who married one of the Macleods in the Fairy Room in the tower, and left it behind when she was summoned back to fairyland twenty years after. Scott, who visited Dunvegan, noted in his diary that the Flag had three properties – 'produced in battle it multiplied the numbers of Macleods; spread on the nuptial bed it ensured fertility; and lastly, it brought herring into the loch'.

The Cuillins from Sligachan, Skye

Sligachan, a small village nine miles south of Portree, is situated at the head of the sea loch of the same name. It cowers beneath the menacing peaks of the Cuillins. There are fifteen of these peaks over 3,000 feet high, and they are a favourite testing-ground for climbers, who do not fear their sheer black precipices and deep corries, often made highly dangerous by the sudden swirling mists.

In the centre of the Cuillins lies Loch Coruisk. The name means 'water cauldron', and the ink-black appearance of this 'loch that never smiles' may remind the imaginative of the contents of a witch's pot.

54

The Sands of Morar, Argyllshire

The sands of Morar Bay, the whitest in Scotland, are framed by rugged headlands, and are separated from Loch Morar by a narrow strip of land. Morar, a fresh-water loch, is some twelve miles long. At one part it is over 1,000 feet deep, and a shapeless monster called 'Morag' is supposed to rise from the depths when a Macdonald dies. It was once the crater of a volcano.

Several miles away is Arisaig, where Macdonald of Morar was the first Highland chief to join Prince Charles Edward on his arrival in 1745. A year later, Macdonald and some other defeated Jacobites took refuge on Eilean Ban, an isle on the loch that had been used as a hiding-place by Catholic priests after the Reformation. They were surprised by Hanoverian troops, but Macdonald and all the others except one escaped. The unlucky one, Simon Fraser of Lovat, was taken to London and executed.

In the Pass of Glencoe, Argyllshire

Glencoe, a gloomy defile between Glen Etive and Ballaculish, was described by Lord Macaulay as 'the very valley of death'. Here, on the night of February 13th, 1692, thirty-eight Macdonalds, including two women and two children, were slaughtered by Government troops whom they had been entertaining for twelve days. Many others perished in their flight through the snow. The Massacre was ordered by Sir John Dalrymple, Under-Secretary of State, because old MacIan, head of the clan, had been slow in taking the oath of allegiance to William of Orange. It is said to have been instigated by the Earl of Breadalbane, a hereditary enemy of the Macdonalds. The story of this tragedy can be read in Marjorie Bowen's novel, *The Glen o' Weeping,* a name that no traveller will forget after viewing this desolate spot and the dreadful memories it evokes.

Glencoe is reputed to have been the birthplace of Ossian.

Inveraray Castle, Argyllshire

Inveraray Castle, on the shores of Loch Fyne, was originally built in the fifteenth century by Campbell of Glenurchy, an ancestor of the houses of Breadalbane and Argyll, and for over 400 years it has been the main residence of successive Earls, Marquises and Dukes of Argyll. The present building was erected in 1745 by one of the Dukes, and it was restored in 1879-1880.

Outside its gates is the town of Inveraray, which has a beautiful old Celtic cross. It was the birthplace of Neil Munro, author of *Doom Castle* and other romantic novels about this district. The trial scene in Stevenson's *Catriona* is laid in the old town.

On the shores of Loch Lomond, Dumbartonshire

Perhaps the best known of all of Scotland's lochs, because of the song about its 'bonnie banks', Lomond is often called 'the Queen of Scottish lakes'. This is partly wrong, since the Lake of Menteith, also in the Trossachs, is the only 'lake' in the country.

Lomond is about twenty-one miles long, stretching southward from Glen Falloch to Balloch, and you can reach it easily from Glasgow. A trip on one of the loch's steamers will show why Tobias Smollett, born in Dumbartonshire in 1721, a surgeon who became a novelist, wrote in *Humphrey Clinker:* 'I have seen the Lago di Garda, Albano di Vico, Bolsena and Geneva, and I prefer Loch Lomond to them all ... Everything here is romantic beyond imagination'.

James Bridie, another doctor who became one of Scotland's most famous playwrights, lived for several years before his death at Drymen, a few miles from the south end of the loch.

Dunure Harbour, Ayrshire

Dunure, or Fisherton, a coastal village eight miles south of Ayr, is in the Parish of Maybole. Its artificial harbour was constructed in 1811 and cost £50,000, but it was neglected, and it is used now only by fishermen.

On a cliff overhanging the harbour are the ruins of Dunure Castle, where in 1570, after a quarrel about some lands, Gilbert Kennedy, Earl of Cassilis, known as 'the King of Carrick', roasted the Abbot of Crossraguel over the great kitchen fire and basted him until the Abbot signed away his claim.

Some miles down the coast is Turnberry, the scene of Robert the Bruce's landing from Arran to fight for the Scottish crown.

Burns' Statue and Greyfriars Church, Dumfries

The largest town in the south of Scotland, Dumfries is famous for its associations with Robert Burns. The tiny house where he died in 1796, his mausoleum in St. Michael's Churchyard, and this statue, unveiled in 1882, are all places of pilgrimage. In the Globe Inn, one of his 'howffs', you can still see two verses that he scratched on a window. But Dumfries' history goes back long before Burns. It was made a Royal Burgh in the twelfth century, and the old bridge spanning the River Nith was built about a hundred years later by the Lady Devorgilla of Galloway, wife of John Balliol, who founded Balliol College, Oxford. Maxwelltown, on the other side of the Nith, used to be an independent village, but it was joined to the Burgh of Dumfries in 1930, and Annie Laurie's braes are now covered by council houses.

Melrose Abbey

Melrose Abbey has been called 'the most precious jewel of the Borders'. It was built by David I in 1136, but as it lay in the way of English invaders, it was despoiled again and again. The ruins you see today are those of the building restored by Robert the Bruce in 1326. Bruce's heart is buried in the Abbey, although his body lies at Dunfermline in Fifeshire.

The River Tweed flows gently past the Abbey and the pleasant little town of Melrose. Three miles away is Abbotsford, the home of Walter Scott, who loved the ruins and wrote:

> *Through slender shafts of shapely stone,*
> *By foliaged tracery combined,*
> *Thou would'st have thought some fairy's hand,*
> *'Twixt poplars straight the osier wand,*
> *In many a freakish knot, had twined;*
> *Then framed a spell, when work was done,*
> *And changed the willow-wreaths to stone.*

68

In the Walter Scott country, with the Eildon Hills

The Eildons lie a mile and a half south of Melrose. Their summits rise from one base, and superstition has it that one hill was split in three in a night by a demon acting on the orders of Michael Scot, the twelfth-century 'Border Wizard', who helped to bring Greek and Oriental knowledge to the western world. Within their valleys, Thomas the Rhymer is supposed to have spent three years with the Queen of the Fairies.

The fires of Druid sacrifices once blazed from their tops, and on the summit of the northern peak are the remains of a Roman encampment and a Caledonian tumulus.

Little wonder, therefore, that Edwin Muir wrote: 'These hills, so large in design and so small in scale, seem to be formed to be the home of fairies and gnomes; and the legends which have gathered round them are a real expression of the natural quality they posses'.

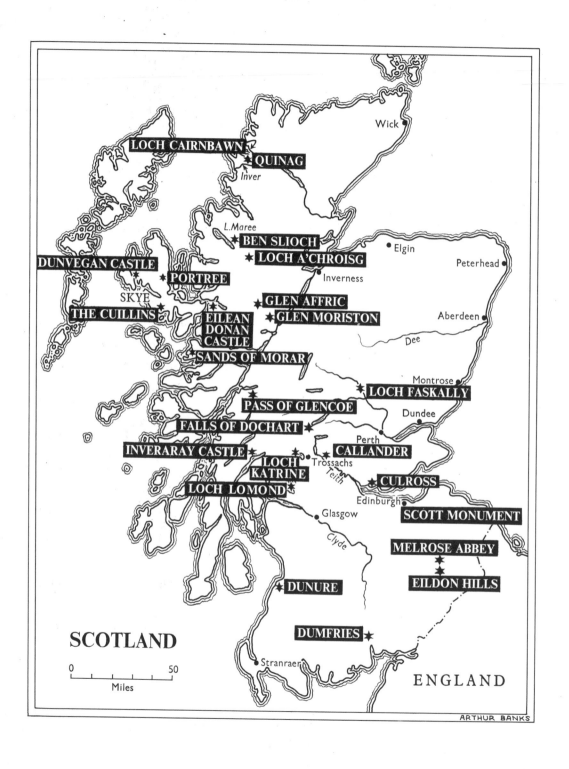

LOCH CAIRNBAWN
QUINAG
Inver

Wick

BEN SLIOCH
L.Maree
LOCH A'CHROISG

Elgin

Peterhead

DUNVEGAN CASTLE
PORTREE
Inverness

SKYE
GLEN AFFRIC
THE CUILLINS
GLEN MORISTON

Aberdeen

EILEAN DONAN CASTLE
Dee
SANDS OF MORAR

Montrose

LOCH FASKALLY

PASS OF GLENCOE
Dundee

FALLS OF DOCHART
Perth
CALLANDER

INVERARAY CASTLE
Trossachs
LOCH KATRINE
Teith

CULROSS

LOCH LOMOND
Edinburgh

SCOTT MONUMENT

Glasgow

Clyde
MELROSE ABBEY

EILDON HILLS

DUNURE

DUMFRIES

SCOTLAND

0   50
Miles

Stranraer

ENGLAND

ARTHUR BANKS